A Note to Parents

DK READERS is a compelling program for beginning readers, designed in conjunctio~~~~ ~~~~ experts, including Dr. Linda G~ Education at Clemson Univers~ served as President of the Nati~ the College Reading Associati~ Reading Association.

Beautiful illustrations and superb full-color photographs combine with engaging, easy-to-read stories to offer a fresh approach to each subject in the series. Each DK READER is guaranteed to capture a child's interest while developing his or her reading skills, general knowledge, and love of reading.

The five levels of DK READERS are aimed at different reading abilities, enabling you to choose the books that are exactly right for your child:

Pre-level 1: Learning to read
Level 1: Beginning to read
Level 2: Beginning to read alone
Level 3: Reading alone
Level 4: Proficient readers

The "normal" age at which a child begins to read can be anywhere from three to eight years old. Adult participation through the lower levels is very helpful for providing encouragement, discussing storylines, and sounding out unfamiliar words.

No matter which level you select, you can be sure that you are helping your child learn to read, then read to learn!

LONDON, NEW YORK, MUNICH,
MELBOURNE, AND DELHI

Editorial Lead Heather Jones
Special Sales Manager Silvia La Greca
Associate Publisher Nigel Duffield

Reading Consultant
Linda Gambrell, Ph.D.

Produced by
Shoreline Publishing Group LLC
President James Buckley, Jr.
Designer Tom Carling, carlingdesign.com

The Boy Scouts of America®, Cub Scouts®,
Boys' Life®, and rank insignia are registered
trademarks of the Boy Scouts of America.
Printed under license from the
Boy Scouts of America.

First American Edition, 2008
08 09 10 11 10 9 8 7 6 5 4 3 2 1
Published in the United States by DK Publishing
375 Hudson Street, New York, New York 10014

Copyright © 2008 Dorling Kindersley Limited

Published in Great Britain by Dorling Kindersley Limited

DK books are available at special discounts when purchased in bulk
for sales promotions, premiums, fund-raising, or educational use.
For details, contact:
DK Publishing Special Markets, 375 Hudson St., New York, NY 10014
SpecialSales@dk.com

A catalog record for this book is available
from the Library of Congress.
ISBN: 9780756644185 (Paperback)

Printed and bound in China by L. Rex Printing Co. LTD.

The publisher would like to thank the following for their kind
permission to reproduce their photographs:
(Key: a=above; b=below/bottom; c=center; l=left; r=right; t=top)
AP/Wide World: 8b, 28bl, 32, 33tr; Dreamstime.com: Danuta Nowacka 16bl;
iStock: 7, 37; NASA: 8tl, 9, 10b, 11t, 11b, 12-13 (all), 14bl, 14b, 15t, 16t, 18t,
19t, 20-21 (all), 22-23 (all), 24-25 (all), 26, 27t, 29t, 29b, 30-31 (all), 34t, 34b,
36t, 36b, 38-39 (all), 40-41 (all), 42, 43t, 45.

All other images © Dorling Kindersley Limited.
For more information see: www.dkimages.com

Discover more at
www.dk.com

Contents

DK READERS

Boys' Life SERIES

Men on the
Moon

Written by James Buckley, Jr.

DK Publishing

Moon shot
French film maker Georges Melies made *A Trip to the Moon* in 1902, from which this famous photo is taken.

Men in the moon
Over the years, the "man" in the Moon has been known as Soma (Hindu), Rona (Maori), and Bunyip (Australian Aborigine).

Goodnight, Moon

Since human beings first looked up into the night sky, they've seen Earth's only neighbor: the Moon. Reflecting light from the Sun, the Moon lights up at night.

Our nearest neighbor in space has always amazed people. They imagined it was the home of gods or that it was alive. People created stories to show how it came to be. They saw shapes in its bright surface that formed "men in the Moon."

People from China, Rome, Greece, and New Zealand told stories of people and gods that they believed explained the Moon. One ancient Chinese tale said there was a rabbit living in the Moon. Another folktale said the Moon was made of green cheese.

In 1865, popular French author Jules Verne wrote a science-fiction novel called *From the Earth to the Moon*. In it, he imagined travelers from Earth launching a rocket, landing on the Moon, and walking around. Yeah, right! Like that could ever happen!

Jules Verne
Born in France, Verne lived from 1828 to 1905. He was one of the most famous science-fiction writers of all time. His books took readers on amazing journeys to space, under the sea, and to the center of the Earth. He also wrote *Around the World in 80 Days*.

5

The Moon is far from a myth, however. It orbits, or circles, around the Earth about once a month. It doesn't change shape, though that's what it looks like. As it orbits, the sunlight hitting it reflects toward us. As it goes around, we see the Moon from different angles. Our view of the Moon changes from a "full" to a "half" to a "crescent" over the course of a month.

The Moon also affects the world's oceans by helping to make tides. The gravity of the Moon literally pulls the ocean waters of the Earth toward itself as it slowly orbits.

Rocky world
Moon rocks brought back by astronauts have shown that the Moon is made not of cheese, but of iron, magnesium, basalt, and other types of minerals.

Tides
This diagram shows how the gravity of the Moon "pulls" the waters of the Earth toward it. As the Moon does its orbit, the tides of Earth change below it.

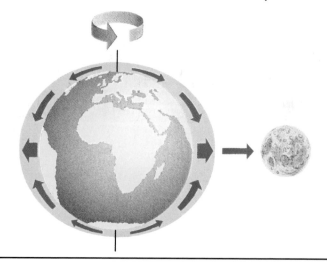

Also, in vast areas of the world, moonlight is many people's only evening illumination.

The Moon has hovered over our world since we began living here, providing light and turning tides. What would it be like, many wondered, to walk on the Moon?

Moon facts:
Size: about one-quarter the size of Earth
Distance: About 240,000 miles (386,000 km) from Earth
Age: about 4.6 billion years

Father of rocketry
American engineer Robert Goddard played a big part in developing early rockets. Working in the 1910s, he sent up small, fuel-powered rockets that were the first baby steps into space.

V2s in London
Sadly, the first uses of rockets like these were for bombs. German V2 rockets exploded in London near the end of World War II.

But how would humans reach the Moon? Science came up with an answer in the 1940s. Near the end of World War II, rockets were used as weapons by German forces. They were developed by rocket engineer Wernher von Braun. But von Braun's real goal was to reach space. Rockets could possibly break through the barrier of gravity. The idea of a rocket that would reach space seemed suddenly much more real.

The United States and the Soviet Union began building rockets and testing them to see how high they could fly. Some did very well,

but many others exploded before reaching space. Building a rocket was a tricky business, but still, scientists began thinking seriously about sending men into space.

At the same time, there was another "war" going on. After World War II, the United States faced a new threat: the Soviet Union (USSR). This mighty empire was seen as a threat by the American government in many areas of life. While the two countries argued over just about everything, they also were

racing against each other to be the first to send men into space. One goal of the "space race" was the Moon.

Baby steps
The first spacecraft from Earth to go near the Moon was Pioneer 4. This space probe flew about 20,000 miles (32,000 km) above the Moon's surface and took the first pictures of it. Soviet craft called Luna were the first to take pictures of the far side of the Moon.

9

First into space

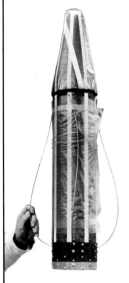

The first "winner" of the space race was the Soviet Union. On October 4, 1957, the Soviets announced that their Sputnik satellite had reached outer space. The news sent shockwaves through the United States. No one could believe that the "enemy" had beaten us into space. The effort to put Americans in space got even bigger.

In 1959, the first group of American astronauts was chosen— the men of the Mercury program. All were pilots, and all went through a tough competition to make the final cut. They began to work feverishly to get a man into space. But once again, the USSR beat

The Soviet satellite Sputnik

Explorer 1
This was the first U.S. satellite. It launched on Jan. 31, 1958.

America to a key milestone. On April 12, 1961, Yuri Gagarin, a "cosmonaut" from the USSR, became the first person to orbit Earth. Three weeks later, Alan Shepard took a 15-minute ride into space to become the first American to leave Earth's gravity.

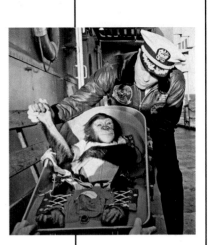

The United States brought in von Braun from Germany to help build bigger, better rockets. He proved to be the right man for the job.

With each side taking giant steps forward (and upward), the space race was in high gear!

Space animals
Before humans were risked in space, animals made the trip. The USSR sent Laika, a dog. American animals included monkeys Able, Baker, and Ham.

Splashdown
Shepard ended his flight in the water— on purpose. His space capsule landed in the Pacific Ocean and was picked up by the U.S. Navy.

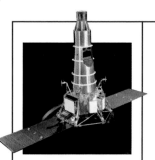

Unmanned
Rangers were the first U.S. spacecraft to reach the Moon in 1961. They took pictures of the Moon's surface.

Amid all the discussion of a space race, one man set the real goal for both sides. In a speech to Congress on May 25, 1961, President John F. Kennedy spoke about the ways that America was great and could be even greater. And he issued a challenge that changed history—to say nothing of lives of U.S. astronauts.

Kennedy said, "I believe that this nation should commit itself to achieving the goal, before the decade is out, of landing a man on the Moon and returning him safely."

It was a bold statement. It rallied America behind the space race.

In February 1962, U.S. astronaut John Glenn put a human face on Kennedy's quest. Glenn became the first person to orbit the Earth.

Kennedy's rallying cry would continue to echo throughout the decade, as U.S. and Soviet space programs raced to find a way to safely land a man on the Moon. The long dream of humanity to reach another world might just come true.

Sadly, Kennedy didn't live to see that dream come true. He was killed by an assassin in November, 1963. However, the men of Apollo kept working to reach Kennedy's goal.

Glenn again
In 1998, John Glenn returned to space. Then a U.S. senator from Ohio, he rode the space shuttle *Discovery*.

LBJ
After Kennedy's death in November, 1963, Lyndon Johnson took over as president. He promised to keep the road to the Moon open.

Lots of wires!
The CM was one of the most complicated machines ever built. It had more than two million parts!

No women?
At the time of the Apollo program, women were not considered ready for space. However, a group of women pilots were chosen and trained as possible astronauts.

Apollo is born

Following Glenn's flight, more and more astronauts—men of the Gemini program—flew into space. Some trips carried probes to examine the Moon. Others tested new spacecraft that astronauts might use for the Moon flights.

The Moon rockets would have two main parts: the command module (CM) and the lunar module (LM). The astronauts would ride in the CM during the several days it took to reach the Moon. Then two of the three crew members would ride down to the lunar surface in the LM. The third astronaut would remain in the CM to pick up the Moon walkers later.

Meanwhile, the Soviets earned another "first" in 1965 with the first space walk. A cosmonaut, tied to his space capsule, floated out into space.

American astronaut Ed White in space

Later in 1965, Ed White became the first American spacewalker.

Though the Apollo program started in 1960, it really got into gear following Kennedy's call. NASA, the U.S. space agency, selected a group of astronauts to form the first Apollo team. Among these men, they all realized, would be the ones who really did it—who really walked on the Moon.

NASA
The American government agency that runs the space program is the National Aeronautics and Space Administration.

The right stuff
A book written by author Tom Wolfe described the process of becoming an astronaut. The book said that all these men had "the right stuff." The phrase has become well known.

Model planes
Many future astronauts enjoyed playing with remote-control model planes. Such planes might have small electric motors.

The Apollo selection process was very hard. But men who loved flight flocked to the join the Apollo team. Many had been fighter pilots. Others were test pilots, civilians who tried out new aircraft. Others, such as Alan Shepard and Gus Grissom, had taken part in earlier space flights. But what made all of them want to take the risks that came with riding rockets into space? One thing all the astronauts had in common was a love of flight.

Michael Collins remembered flying balsa-wood airplane models as kid.

Also, the idea of space flight was still new and mysterious. Kids today are not that impressed watching a space shuttle take off. But in the 1960s, being an astronaut was about the coolest thing a person could be.

"When I heard about the astronaut program, I immediately thought, 'How can I get that job?'" remembered Alan Bean.

When the process was over, NASA had its men for the Moon.

Astro boys
Kids across America played with many toys inspired by astronauts.

Gus Grissom
A trained engineer, Grissom (left) had been to space in a Mercury flight and in command of Gemini 3.

Live TV
During Apollo 7, for the first time, people could see live TV images from a spacecraft. The link between TV and the space race was cemented even further.

Apollo flies

The baby steps to the Moon begin with test flights that sent back pictures and information. Throughout 1965 and 1966, rockets roared into space to test equipment and new ways of living in space.

As all the astronauts knew, flying into space was a risky business. Many were former test pilots who loved the power of the machines they were riding. Sadly, the Apollo era kicked off with a tragedy on a mission that never left the ground.

During a test for what would later be called Apollo 1, three astronauts were killed when fire swept through the CM. Locked in their space suits in a tiny area, they had no escape. Gus Grissom, Ed White, and Roger Chaffee were the first Americans to lose their lives in the attempt to reach the Moon. They would not be the last people lost in the ongoing quest to explore space.

The goal of the Moon remained, despite the tragedy. The men of Apollo pressed on, remembering their friends but also learning from the accident.

In October 1968, Apollo 7 became the first manned Apollo flight. Wally Schirra, Donn Eisele, and Walter Cunningham orbited Earth 163 times to test out the conditions on board the CM.

Other space tragedies
The space shuttle has successfully carried astronauts from dozens of countries into orbit. However, two have ended sadly. In 1987, *Challenger* exploded during takeoff, killing seven astronauts. In 2003, *Columbia* (above) broke up during re-entry, ending the mission and the lives of seven others.

Frank Borman
Frank Borman commanded Apollo 8. He later became a very successful businessman, leading Eastern Airlines for many years.

Fun names
The astronauts named all their spacecraft. For Apollo 10, the CM was "Charlie Brown," while the smaller LM was "Snoopy."

Apollo 8 was supposed to be just another Earth-orbit equipment test. But news that the Soviets might be trying to reach the Moon made NASA change its plans. Apollo 8 would go to the Moon.

Apollo 8 blasted off on Dec. 21, 1968. Three days later, on Christmas Eve, three Apollo astronauts— Frank Borman, James Lovell, and William Anders—became the first men to orbit the Moon. They took amazing color pictures and brought back the first eyewitness descriptions of the surface of the Moon.

Apollo 9 and 10 followed early in 1969. They carried the first models of the "lunar module," the craft that would carry astronauts to the Moon. Apollo 10 carried the LM only nine miles above the Moon. Human beings had never been closer, but there was one giant step left to go.

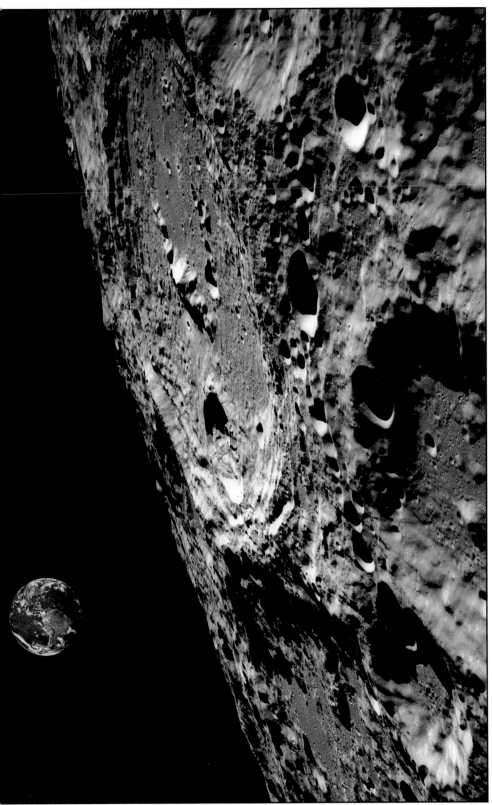

One small step…

Houston
The Apollo flights took off from Florida, but they were controlled from the NASA Space Center in Houston, Texas. It was later named after President Lyndon Johnson.

By early 1969, NASA was ready to make the final giant leap to the Moon. Remember, Kennedy's goal was "by the end of the decade." Now that long-sought goal was just a few months away. They had to hurry.

Three crews of three Apollo astronauts each began tough training for the mission. The crew

of Neil Armstrong, Edwin "Buzz" Aldrin, and Michael Collins was chosen to be the first to attempt a Moon landing.

Either Aldrin or Armstrong would be first on the Moon. Collins would pilot the CM around the Moon as the other two landed. As he orbited the Moon alone, Collins would be, as some called him, "the loneliest man in the universe." He would be in the pitch-dark of the side of the Moon away from the Sun for several hours.

"I was just fine being alone," Collins remembered later. "Plus I had those folks in Houston to talk to."

The plan was that the LM would blast off from the Moon and Collins would then link up it. The trio would then return safely to Earth . . . they hoped.

Space merger
The CM had to link up carefully to the LM. Connecting the two while flying high above the Moon was a very tricky job, but Collins did it perfectly.

Michael Collins
Collins was a West Point graduate and former Air Force test pilot. On Gemini 10 in 1966, he practiced the docking move he later did on Apollo 11.

Lunar module practice
Armstrong practiced on the Lunar Landing Research Vehicle (LLRV). During one flight, he had to bail out of it before it crashed. "He was the coolest guy I knew under pressure," said Apollo astronaut Charles Duke.

Meanwhile, the other two astronauts knew they would be attempting something historic. Since humans had first looked up at the Moon, we had wondered what it would be like up there. Painters created scenes of what they might find. Novelists created Moon bases and exciting adventures.

But for Armstrong and Aldrin, it would be real. They were going to do it.

The two brought different skills to the trip. Armstrong was a fantastic pilot. He had flown the X-15 rocket plane (at right) more than 4,000 miles (6,400 km) per hour. He was able to pilot more than 200 different types of aircraft. Armstrong was not going to be overwhelmed by the mission.

Edwin "Buzz" Aldrin
A graduate of West Point, Aldrin was the only Apollo astronaut with a doctorate in aeronautics. His first trip to space was in Gemini 12. After leaving NASA, he worked in the aviation field, but also continues to promote manned space travel.

Aldrin was more of a scientist, with degrees in aeronautics (the study of flight) and a Ph.D., the highest level of academic work. He was also a pilot, though, having flown F-86s during combat in Korea. Aldrin's combination of knowledge and experience were a perfect pair with Armstrong's piloting and leadership skills.

Together, the two headed off into history.

Neil Armstrong
Humble, quiet, and private, the first man on the Moon grew up in Ohio. He flew Navy fighter pilots during the Korean War. He became an astronaut in 1962 and first went to space on Gemini 8 in 1966. Following his Moon trip, he worked for NASA and later was a teacher at the University of Cincinnati. Armstrong now lives on a farm in Ohio.

The world was watching on TV as the the historic flight approached.

Aldrin noticed something surprising right from the start. "The [normally busy] launch pad was deserted," he said in a 2007 movie.

The liftoff was perfect and a few days later, the crew reached its orbit around the Moon. The LM separated and headed for the Moon.

Fellow astronaut Charles Duke was on the radio with Armstrong. As the "capsule communicator," or "capcom," only Duke would speak with the crew during the flight.

Duke and Armstrong used many technical terms. When Duke said, "Go for PDI," that meant controllers showed that it was safe to "power" the Eagle LM to the surface.

Armstrong and Aldrin soared along above the Moon, aiming for their landing site.

Nixon
In case of disaster, President Nixon pre-recorded a message to the world saying that the astronauts could not make it back to Earth.

Radio
Powerful radios sent signals into space to keep the controllers in touch with the astronauts.

On the Moon

Forever prints
With no wind on the Moon, anything on the surface will remain unchanged. Thus, the first footprints made by Armstrong are probably still up there.

The world watches
These people in Russia were among the 1 billion who watched live as Armstrong stepped onto the Moon.

Just moments before Eagle touched down, an alarm sounded. "We've got a 1202 alarm," Armstrong calmly reported. The computers were overloaded. The problem was soon fixed. Then came another problem. As they looked toward the landing site, they saw large boulders. If the LM landed on a boulder and tipped over, they would be stuck on the Moon.

As the final 60 seconds ticked down, Armstrong took control. Slowly, he lowered the craft to a safe landing.

"Touchdown," he said. "Houston, the Eagle has landed."

After a few hours checking out their gear, it was time to step out into the unknown. For the first time, a human being would touch an alien world.

Flag on Moon
Six U.S. flags still stand on the Moon. They don't fly in the wind, however. To keep the flags up, the astronauts used sticks; otherwise, the flags would hang limply in the windless Moon.

Armstrong was first. As he reached the bottom step, he was watched by more than a billion people live on TV from a camera mounted outside the LM. As his foot touched the lunar surface on July 20, 1969, he said words that will live as long as people look up at the Moon: "That's one small step for a man . . . one giant leap for mankind."

The world united in joy as Armstrong, and later Aldrin, became the first Moon visitors.

A very long-distance call
President Richard Nixon spoke with the astronauts on the Moon, thanking them on behalf of the people back on Earth.

Apollo 12

While the Apollo 11 astronauts went around the world on a tour, other astronauts were excited to take their turns at walking on the Moon. With the safe return of Apollo 11, the space race was over . . . and a new race began, but this was among Apollo astronauts eager to follow their fellow Americans to the Moon.

World tour
While Apollo 12 readied for its flight, the Apollo 11 crew toured the world. The crew spent five weeks visiting dozens of countries, where they were received as heroes.

Moonball?
The CM on Apollo 12 was called the Yankee Clipper. That name came from a type of sailing ship used in the 1800s. It was also the nickname of the great Yankees outfielder Joe DiMaggio.

The Apollo 12 crew was Pete Conrad, Alan Bean, and CM pilot Richard Gordon. Their mission lifted off on November 14, 1969.

With NASA's ability to land and return from the moon settled by Apollo 11, astronauts on later missions focused more on science. A limited amount of air gave them just a few hours at a time on the Moon's surface. "We had to work as fast as we safely could," said Bean. "Every minute was planned out."

That's not to say they didn't have fun. All the Apollo astronauts took time to marvel at their temporary home. Though all were dedicated scientists, they were awestruck to be in such a remote and beautiful place.

But soon, Apollo 12 was back to work, gathering more than 70 pounds (32 kg) of Moon materials.

Pete Conrad
A native of Philadelphia, Conrad was a test pilot in the Navy. He flew on two Gemini missions and after Apollo 12, he was commander of Skylab II, an orbiting space station.

Alan Bean
After Bean left NASA in 1975, he became a well-known artist. Many of his paintings were of lunar scenes.

James Lovell
This Naval Academy graduate and Eagle Scout became a hero to pilots everywhere for his calm under pressure. Apollo 13 was Lovell's fourth flight into space.

TV hit
Famous actor Tom Hanks, a longtime fan of space, helped make and starred in a popular movie about the Apollo 13 flight. Released in 1995, the film is available on DVD.

Apollo 13

The first two manned missions to the Moon had gone off almost perfectly. That streak ended with the unlucky Apollo 13.

About 56 hours into their flight to the Moon, a small explosion rocked the craft. "Houston," mission commander James Lovell calmly reported, "we've had a problem."

An oxygen tank on the CM had blown out, releasing precious air into space. The men had to come home—fast. It was a desperate situation. With little air and power dropping, it was a race to find out a way to get back safely.

Mission Control worked feverishly to find an answer. The best solution: Use the LM as a "lifeboat." But the LM was not built to carry three men for three days.

The crew moved into the tiny LM.

To get enough speed to come home, they actually guided the LM in a "slingshot" move around the Moon.

For the three days the men drifted home, the world waited, tense and worried. Finally, on April 17, the capsule made it back to Earth. It was a stunning moment, a symbol of the astronaut's bravery and NASA's problem-solving ability.

Walter Cronkite
CBS newsman Walter Cronkite reported live, with help from space experts, during the Apollo 11 launch and throughout the Apollo 13 near-disaster.

Heading home
After splashdown, orange life rings and bubble-like buoys kept the capsules from sinking. The astronauts were lifted into helicopters in baskets.

Apollo 14

Following the near-disaster of Apollo 13, there was some discussion of scaling back Apollo. But NASA decided to continue the flights. Its next flight got as much attention on the sports page as the front page.

Alan Shepard, the first American in space in 1961, was the Apollo 14 commander. He was also a big fan

Alan Shepard
One of the most experienced astronauts, Shepard became an astronaut in 1959 after 12 years flying jets for the Navy. In 1961 he made the first American trip to space. He spent the rest of the decade as the head of the NASA Astronaut Office before making his second trip to space in Apollo 14.

of golf. He worked with an engineer to create a stick with the head of a six-iron on it. During one of his walks on the Moon, he put down a golf ball and then got out that special tool. Shepard became the first golfer in space!

Together, Shepard and Edgar Mitchell also used the MET (shown at left), or modular equipment transport. It was basically the first wheelbarrow in space, used to carry the astronauts' gear on the Moon.

Mitchell had an amazing experience on the flight back. He said later that he felt that he was back in the stars that had made us all. He sensed that he was once again merging with "the same molecules" that formed everything in the universe. Many astronauts reported getting new senses of peace and calm from their time in space.

Iron play
Shepard used the head of a six-iron for his historic shot. This kind of golf club has a slight angle so the ball rises after being hit.

Edgar Mitchell
Navy test pilot Mitchell joined NASA in 1966. His only space flight was Apollo 14. His experiences in space changed his life. He left NASA to study the human mind and space. He often speaks about how space deeply affected him.

Apollo 15

James Irwin
A native of Pennsylvania and an Air Force pilot, Irwin was a top test pilot. He joined NASA in 1966 and made his only space flight on Apollo 15.

While the first three Apollo crews stayed near the LM, Apollo 15's men explored! They didn't walk, however . . . they drove.

Using a special "lunar rover," the astronauts could take a Sunday drive 240,000 miles from the nearest gas station.

"At every bounce, you actually left the surface of

the Moon a little bit," said Harrison Schmitt, who would drive the rover for Apollo 17.

"I sure felt safe driving it," John Young said. "There was no traffic!"

The lunar rover would be used on two more Apollo trips. It was powered by just a few batteries and could go as fast as eight miles (12 km) per hour. It allowed the astronauts to cover large areas of the Moon, taking pictures and gathering samples.

Rover wheels
Rubber tires filled with air would have popped in the low gravity of the Moon. The rover's wheels were instead made of wire mesh with small spike-like cleats to help with traction.

How big?
The lunar rover was about as big as a Volkswagen Beetle. The rover folded up to be attached to the outside of the LM for takeoff and landing.

David Scott
After growing up in Texas, Scott became an Air Force pilot, serving in Europe. He joined the astronaut corps in 1963 and made flights to space on Gemini 8, Apollo 9, and Apollo 15.

Genesis rock
Scott found a rock that scientists later said was 4.5 billion years old. Did it date from the beginning of the solar system?

One Apollo 15 astronaut had a special experience. As David Scott went through the careful notebook of checklists given to him by NASA, he got a few surprises. His children and his wife had written notes that were put in the notebook. He got good wishes from his young sons thousands of miles up in space.

After he returned, Scott, like the other astronauts, tried to describe what he had seen on the Moon.

"It was like a beautiful desert," he said. "There was so much excitement and wonder at seeing it."

Apollo 15's crew saw a very different part of the Moon. The landing area was a flat plain surrounded by high mountains. The highest measured more than 14,000 feet (4,267 m). Down below, one edge of the plain dropped off into an interesting canyon-like formation.

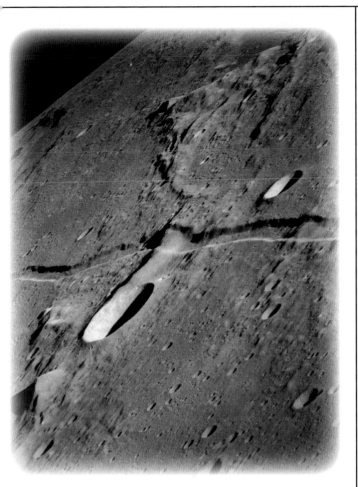

Moon-ellite
While Scott and Irwin worked below, Al Worden flew around the Moon in the CM. He photographed moonscapes and released the first permanent lunar satellite.

Navy help
Like most Apollo missions, Apollo 15 ended after the capsule was pulled from the ocean by ships and men from the U.S. Navy.

This was the Hadley Rille (above), more than 1,300 feet (396 m) deep. The astronauts went to the edge and looked down. The view was awesome, but they would have to leave visiting the bottom for future lunar explorers. It was time to go home.

Oops! Astronauts are not perfect. During a moon walk, Young accidentally caught his boot on a cable from a piece of experiment gear. The cable ripped out, making the experiment impossible.

Apollo 16

In April 1972, Apollo 16 headed for the Moon to find evidence of volcanoes. After looking for more than 70 hours, they came up with nothing. The Moon looked like it did thanks to meteors, not volcanoes.

Meanwhile, Charlie Duke and John Young, like the Apollo

men before them, had to adapt to working in a low-gravity environment. Their bodies weighed only one-sixth as much as they did on earth. Learning to move safely and easily took practice, first on Earth, then on the Moon.

"We adapted quickly," said Charlie Duke. "John [Young] could race around like a gazelle. I moved sort of like a waddling duck."

Duke took a famous photo of Young saluting while leaping three feet off the ground (left)!

After finding his "moon legs," Duke did make it around fairly easily. Like others, he took a moment to reflect during his time on the Moon. He took out a picture of his family. He put it on the surface, where it remains today. "Who will find this picture?" he wondered years later.

John Young
Few human beings have been in space as often as Young. The former Navy test pilot first flew on Gemini 3. He later was on Gemini 10 and Apollo 10. He walked on the Moon during Apollo 16. Later, he was aboard the first flight of the Space Shuttle as well as Spacelab. He headed the Astronaut Office until 1987.

Apollo 17

After more than three years, billions of dollars, and hundreds of hours of space flight, man's visits to the Moon ended after this final Apollo mission. Commander Gene Cernan and Harrison Schmitt, a geologist, drove the lunar rover for 19 miles and explored many new areas. The two camped on the Moon for three days, spending 22 hours out of the LM. Schmitt collected more than 200 pounds (90 kg) of material for later study, carefully using tools to pick them up.

Cernan raised the American flag on the Moon for the final time. He used the actual flag from back home in Mission Control where it had flown since 1966.

"I called the Moon my home for three days," Cernan later said. Through 2008, only 11 other men

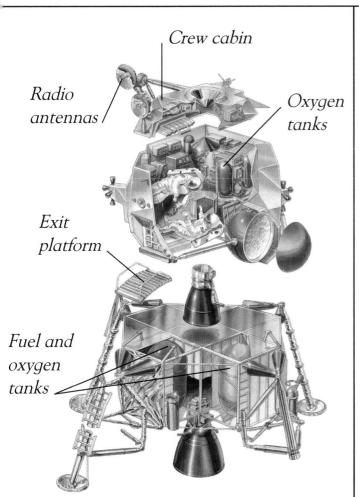

Crew cabin

Radio antennas

Oxygen tanks

Exit platform

Fuel and oxygen tanks

This shows how the Apollo LM (top) and CM fit together.

Eugene Cernan
A Navy pilot, he joined NASA in 1963 and made three space flights. He was later a businessman and often was on TV helping viewers understand space shuttle launches.

Last words
Said by Cernan, the final words from the Moon (so far!) were, "America's challenge of today has forged man's destiny of tomorrow."

could say that. Cernan's were the last footprints made on the Moon . . . so far.

Apollo 17 blasted off from the Moon on December 15, 1972. The Apollo missions were completed. No one has been back since.

White suits
Why are spacesuits white? To reflect the powerful rays of the Sun. Unprotected by atmosphere, astronauts need protection. The suits cool them with water flowing through tubes, while the white fabric deflects some heat.

What's next?

NASA launched a new program in 2005 aimed at sending astronauts back to the Moon. The massive Ares rocket will carry Orion astronauts. The Ares will be a cargo rocket filled with material that might be used to build a more permanent space station on the Moon's surface. The first Orion flight is scheduled for 2015.

Will that lead to human beings living on the Moon? That's not very likely. With no atmosphere and only one-sixth the gravity, the Moon is a not a human-friendly place. However, as a temporary home for scientists studying space, it just might be perfect. Telescopes on the Moon could see farther into space than any on or orbiting Earth.

For the astronauts who have actually been there already,

r, their memories remain
. They are still the only
ns who have visited another
f our universe.

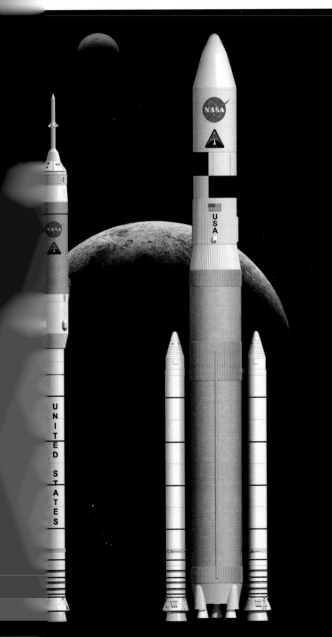

45

Moon base
Will we ever live on the moon? Setting up a moon base is one the long-term drawing board for NASA, but no firm plans exist for now. But who knows? Maybe you'll be the first visitor!

Memories
"Not a day goes by," said Apollo 12's Alan Bean, "that I don't think about my time on the Moon and realize just how special that really was." Buzz Aldrin looks to the future: "There is so much more to explore!"

Find out more
Books

Eyewitness: Space Exploration
by Carole Stott
(DK Publishing, 2004)
This book is packed with pictures of rockets, astronauts, space capsules, satellites, and even space food! Find out how human beings have figured out how to explore and even live in space.

Reaching for the Moon
by Buzz Aldrin
Why not hear it right from a Moon walker? Buzz Aldrin of Apollo 11 tells his amazing story in this book. Read how he dreamed of space travel, and then worked hard to make his dreams come true.

Space Exploration
by Ron Miller
(Twenty-First Century Books, 2007)
Focusing on how human beings got from down here to "up there," this book tracks space travel from the first rockets to the space shuttle. Learn more about how rockets were invented and how they have made space travel possible.

Web sites

Boys' Life Magazine
www.boyslife.org
Visit the official site of this cool magazine and search for
articles and stories about astronauts, space, and rockets.

Go the source!
www.nasa.gov/audience/forstudents/index.html
Space fans beware: You can get lost for hours in this
awesome site, which has thousands of pages on NASA
history, the entire Apollo program, the space shuttles, and
much more. This site is aimed at students your age. There is
also a NASA Kids' Club with games and other stories.

Take a walk on the Moon
**www.smithsonianeducation.org/students/idealabs/
walking_on_the_moon.html**
The Smithsonian Institute's Air & Space Museum made this
Web site to help kids learn more about Moon exploration.
A cool video takes viewers step-by-step through an Apollo
mission. There are hundreds of photos ,too.

*Note to Parents: These Web sites are not endorsed by Boy Scouts of America or DK Publishing and have
not been completely examined. However, at press time, they provided the sort of information described.
Internet experts always suggest that you work with your children to help them understand how to safely
navigate the Web.*

Bonus!
http://www.scouting.org/Media/FactSheets/02-558.aspx
See a list of all the U.S. astronauts who were Boy Scouts!

Glossary

Aeronautics
The study of flight.

Atmosphere
The gases that surround the Earth.

Command module
The portion of the two-part Apollo spacecraft in which the astronauts rode to and from the Moon.

Cosmonaut
A space traveler from the Soviet Union.

Engineer
A scientist who figures out how mechanical or electronic things work.

Folktale
A story told for many years, often used to explain things in nature.

Geologist
A scientist who studies the Earth and what it is made of.

Gravity
The force that binds all objects to the Earth.

Liftoff
When a rocket shoots off the Earth and enters outer space.

Lunar
Anything having to do with the Moon.

Lunar module
The portion of the two-part Apollo spacecraft that goes to and from the Moon itself.

Mission Control
The controller headquarters for NASA space flights, located in Houston, Texas.

Modular
Made up of several parts.

NASA
The National Aeronautics and Space Administration, the U.S. agency that organizes and runs all American space missions.

Rille
A very deep canyon or cut into the land.

Satellite
An object that orbits another object.

Spacelab
A large space station built and flown in the 1970s; astronauts lived on board the station for many months, performing experiments.

Space race
The competition between the United States and the Soviet Union to get the first space travelers to the Moon.

Splashdown
The end of a space flight that occurs when the capsule, floating down beneath parachutes, lands in the ocean to be recovered by aircraft and ships.